# KEYBOARD SUITES

## DIETRICH BUXTEHUDE

DOVER PUBLICATIONS
Garden City, New York

# CONTENTS

*Bibliographical Note*

This Dover edition, first published in 2002, is a compilation of nineteen keyboard works originally published in an authoritative early edition.

*International Standard Book Number*

*ISBN-13: 978-0-486-42045-5*
*ISBN-10: 0-486-42045-0*

Manufactured in the United States of America
42045008
www.doverpublications.com

# Suite I in C major

**Allemande**

## Courante

# Sarabande

Gigue

# Suite II in C major

**Allemande**

## Courante

## Sarabande

**Gigue**

# Suite III in C major

**Allemande**

**Courante**

**Sarabande**

**Double**

**Gigue**

# Suite IV in C major

**Allemande**

**Courante**

**Sarabande**

# Suite V in C major

**Allemande**

**Courante**

**Sarabande**

# Gigue

# Suite VI in D minor

**Allemande d'Amour**

**Courante**

Sarabande d'Amour

**Sarabande**

**Gigue**

# Suite VII in D minor

**Allemande**

**Double**

## Courante

# Double

## Sarabande

## Sarabande

# Suite VIII in D minor

**Allemande**

**Courante**

Sarabande

# Gigue

# Suite IX in D major

**Allemande**

## Courante

# Suite X in E minor

**Allemande**

# Courante

Sarabande

# Gigue

# Suite XI in E minor

**Allemande**

## Courante

## Sarabande

Gigue

# Suite XII in E minor

Allemande

**Courante**

**Sarabande**

**Sarabande**

**Gigue**

# Suite XIII in F major

**Allemande**

Courante

Sarabande

Gigue

# Suite XIV in G minor

**Allemande**

# Courante

**Sarabande**

**Gigue**

# Suite XV in G minor

**Allemande**

**Courante**

**Sarabande**

**Gigue**

# Suite XVI in G minor

**Allemande**

**Courante**

**Sarabande**

# Gigue

# Suite XVII in G major

**Allemande**

## Courante

## Sarabande

## Gigue

# Suite XVIII in A minor

**Allemande**

**Courante**

**Sarabande**

Gigue

# Suite XIX in A major

Allemande

**Courante**

**Sarabande**

Gigue